SCHIRMER
PERFORMANCE
EDITIONS

GURLITT
ALBUMLEAVES FOR THE YOUNG
Opus 101
Twenty Little Pieces for Piano

Edited and Recorded by Margaret Otwell

To access companion recorded performances online, visit:
www.halleonard.com/mylibrary

Enter Code
5622-9274-6238-7277

On the cover:
Children's Round
by Hans Thoma
(1839-1924)

ISBN 978-1-4234-0367-8

G. SCHIRMER, Inc.

DISTRIBUTED BY

HAL•LEONARD®
7777 W. BLUEMOUND RD. P.O. BOX 13819 MILWAUKEE, WI 53213

www.musicsalesclassical.com
www.halleonard.com

CONTENTS

The price of this publication includes access to companion recorded performances online, for download or streaming, using the unique code found on the title page. Visit **www.halleonard.com/mylibrary** and enter the access code.

HISTORICAL NOTES

CORNELIUS GURLITT (1820-1901)

Cornelius Gurlitt was a man in the right place at the right time. As a composer of piano music who was most noted for his miniatures, or character pieces, he had the great good fortune to live during the era in which the piano became the most popular form of home entertainment and the public appetite for piano music could not be satisfied.

Born in Altona, Prussia, on February 10, 1820, Cornelius Gurlitt arrived in this world at the height of the first industrial revolution that swept through Britain, Europe, and the United States. This was a period of mechanization and technological invention that made mass production of goods possible for the first time in history. Workers were freed from back-breaking labor and could, by learning the skills of operating the newly invented machinery, be more productive and earn more money than ever possible before. Their money created a new demand for consumer goods, which fueled the factories to produce even more. This in turn caused industrialized economies to grow at never-before-seen rates. The prosperity of the age created an enormous middle class—in fact it made the middle class the largest class in industrialized nations of that time.

The popularity of the piano is tied to the birth of the middle class during this historic period. In previous generations, owning a piano was a privilege of wealthy aristocrats. Playing the piano was a social skill reserved for those with both money and tremendous amounts of leisure time. The working class of the era had neither. But by the early decades of the 1800s, families of the swelling middle class did have the money to buy pianos, particularly upright pianos that cost far less than traditional grand pianos. They also had the money to pay for lessons and to buy music.

Even if the adults who became members of the growing middle class didn't learn to play the piano, they saw to it that their children had the opportunity to learn to play. They wanted a piano in their parlor, partly as a mark of social status or achievement, and partly as a source of entertainment.

Piano miniatures such as the ones written by Cornelius Gurlitt were wildly popular as children's pieces, parlor pieces, or entertaining little tunes that people could play at gatherings of friends and family. Although countless such pieces existed at the height of the era, only the finest of them remain in print today, more than a century after they were written. Robert Schumann (1810-56) wrote a lovely book of miniatures, the most famous of such collections, that was published as his *Album for the Young.*

Many of Gurlitt's piano works have colorful, descriptive names like "Grossvaters Geburtstag" (Grandfather's Birthday) or Salto Mortale (Aerial Somersault) and "Heiterer Morgen" (A Sunshiny Morning). His vivid titles are no surprise given his lifelong interest in art. His brother Louis was a very successful artist whose paintings are still held in high regard. Cornelius himself studied painting in Rome and was known to have created some fine paintings. He also studied music in Rome, where he was nominated an honorary member of the papal academy "Di Santa Cecilia" and graduated as "Professor of Music." His earlier studies were in Leipzig, where he studied with Karl Reineke, and in Copenhagen. Gurlitt worked as a pianist and church organist, and also served as a military band master for a time. He wrote music in a number of different genres, including symphonies, songs, operas, cantatas, and educational keyboard pieces. He died in his hometown of Altona on June 17, 1901.

—Elaine Schmidt

PERFORMANCE NOTES

Gurlitt's exquisite talent for the miniature reveals itself in each of the charming piano solos in this collection. His descriptive titles, playful characterizations, and finely crafted scenes draw the performer into a child's innocent and imaginative world. Many of the pieces have titles and characteristics reminiscent of Schumann's more famous collection for children, *The Album for the Young*, written in 1848. Although I found no direct evidence that would prove Gurlitt's *Albumleaves* were directly inspired by Schumann's collection, the obvious parallels, particularly in the choice of titles, reveal a striking connection to Schumann's own *Album*. It is quite possible that Schumann's *characterstücke* did influence Gurlitt's collection. The two composers knew each other and shared a mutual friend in Niels Gade, the Norwegian composer.

The technical level of Gurlitt's pieces closely resembles the easier solos in the first half of Schumann's collection of solos, but it is there that the two composers part company. The piano solos in the second half of Schumann's *Album for the Young* exhibit a burgeoning virtuosity that Gurlitt's solos do not aspire to, although the pieces in his collection are also progressive. Gurlitt's character pieces are more accessible to less skillful players and younger students, and thus can serve as an excellent springboard to Schumann's more complex character pieces. Yet Gurlitt's lovely piano solos may be savored for their own unique qualities as well. They are charming, finely crafted miniatures that all pianists will enjoy discovering and performing.

Notes on this Edition

I have used Louis Köhler's edition in Schirmer's *Library of Piano Classics*, Volume 309 (1895), as a score source for this new edition; no extant manuscript source exists for comparison. The Schirmer score contains few slurs, articulation, or other interpretive markings; it also entirely lacks pedal indications. It is possible that these sparse editorial details are Gurlitt's own and that Köhler transcribed them faithfully. I have elected to include all the editorial details found in the Schirmer Library edition, adding a few others for consistency, or where some editorial direction or pedaling would be helpful to the overall interpretation of a piece. These added slurs or articulations are bracketed in the score and any editorial pedal is indicated with a dotted line.

If the details in the source edition are Gurlitt's, the relative scarcity of interpretive or instructional details is somewhat surprising, for if these solos were written for students one would expect to find more instructive markings throughout. The titles for individual pieces in the set also suggest that Gurlitt may have written them for young children. However, biographical sources do not mention that he taught extensively, so it may be that, like Schumann, he merely sought to capture a childlike spirit in these solos but wrote them for more skillful pianists who could readily add their own personal nuances to them in performance.

Even so, the charming lyricism and straightforward harmonic structure of these solos make them ideal Romantic-period pieces for the novice pianist to study. These lovely pieces require only a good imagination to make them come alive, and their technical demands do not go beyond an intermediate student's playing abilities. Those who may want a detailed performance model will find one in my own performances on the CD included with the score. I have also given some interpretive suggestions for individual pieces in the notes that follow. These miniatures can embrace a wide range of expressive ideas, all of which may be valid. By not overly editing the present score, I hope to encourage performers to approach these lovely pieces with a free, imaginative spirit. Performances are most convincing when the pianist develops an interpretation based on his or her own thoughtful and deeply felt ideas.

Notes on the Individual Pieces

Marsch (March)

Gurlitt opens his collection with a tuneful, outgoing march in the bright key of D Major, a fitting way to begin a set of piano solos dedicated to youthful pianists. Playing soldier remains a favorite imaginative pastime for most children, and it is easy to picture a child marching along to this straightforward, captivating melody. The recurring first theme clearly suggests a lively fife-and-drum band. A steady beat and sprightly touch will give the opening phrases a cheerful, playful character. Performers should give careful attention to the two-note slurs in the contrasting phrase at mm. 9-12. These slurs extend over the bar, an important detail that younger students may overlook. Observing these slurs while also playing the remaining notes in these measures slightly *non-legato* adds expressive detail to one's performance. The slurs over the bar also help propel this new phrase forward with a broader horizontal sweep than the two preceding phrases.

Morgengebet (Morning Prayer)

This serene piece is an excellent study in playing three voices simultaneously. Perhaps mindful of a younger student's limitations, Gurlitt assigns the left hand a single voice most of the time, while the right hand, almost always the stronger hand for most novice pianists, must play two. All three voices combine in a prayerful song in chorale style. Slurs are not used here to emphasize the *legato* quality of the phrasing, nor is pedal indicated, but the style of this chorale obviously calls for pedal, changing with the harmonic progressions, and more accomplished pianists should enhance the seamless phrasing by employing finger-legato as well. The lower-voice quarter notes in the right hand, especially, should be played with a clinging touch. These passing tones enrich the melodic line, filling it out with a gentle counterpoint. Later in the collection, two other solos require a more sophisticated use of finger-legato with finger substitutions. This piece, therefore, serves as a good introduction to skills that return later in a more challenging form.

Heiterer Morgen (A Sunshiny Morning)

The phrases in this cheerful piece in 3/4 meter always begin on the third beat of the measure. It is important to ease into each phrase gently, being careful not to accent the initial note, and to give a slightly accented pulse to the downbeats. A dotted-eighth/16th-note rhythm figures prominently throughout the piece, making this solo an effective study in rhythmic precision as well.

Nordische Klänge (Northern Strains)

The opening bars of this turbulent solo quickly set the scene with insistent left-hand chords lending urgency to the melody, imparting an almost anxious feeling to the entire section. Gurlitt marks this opening "*marcato molto,*" further emphasizing the unsettled mood. The left-hand repeated notes must be played close to the keys with a kind of intense rhythmic precision, and with a determined pulse that sweeps the melody along. Pedal should be used sparingly, and I recommend only a surface pedal that releases on beat two. Although the right-hand melody has no slurs, I suggest playing it in a "rough" *legato*, in two complementary four-bar phrases. This stormy opening and its return at the end of the piece frame a very brief, sunnier interlude whose short, skipping phrases, punctuated by strong *sf* accents, have the distinct flavor of a folk dance.

In this piece, as well as a later one ("Türkischer Marsch"), the ending of the second part is marked with a repeat sign, but there is no corresponding sign to indicate where this repeat begins. This could have been an editorial lapse in the source edition, but also may have been Gurlitt's own omission in his original score. We have chosen to add an editorial repeat at the start of the second part in both solos.

An der Quelle (By the Spring)

The steady, fluid eighth notes in the left-hand accompaniment aptly convey the imagery of the title. Set against this accompaniment, a gentle, lilting melody made up primarily of rising or falling two-note slurs and regular eight-bar periods flows along with elegant ease. It is important to observe carefully the eighth-note rests in the melody; *legato* pedaling, which can be used freely throughout, should not obscure this lovely melodic detail. Note how Gurlitt stretches out the indication *perdendosi* over mm. 36 and 37 to emphasize the gradual nature of the *diminuendo* to *pp* here.

Schlummerlied (Lullaby)

The elegant simplicity of this peaceful lullaby makes it an ideal expressive solo for intermediate-level students. "Lullaby" bears a striking resemblance to the piece titled "Melody" in Schumann's *Album for the Young*, but Gurlitt places this piece in the key of D major, whereas Schumann kept his solo in the easier key of C major. Just as in "By the Spring," which immediately precedes this work, the left hand plays an important role as the constant eighth-note foundation against which a gentle melody unfolds. But here the left hand also has a melodic component: the eighth notes on the first part of each beat form a duet with the right-hand melody. Students will hear this duet readily if they practice the phrases hands together, playing only each moving note in the left-hand accompaniment with its right-hand partner.

Schlummerlied, Opus 101, No. 6: mm. 1-3

Studying "By the Spring" and "Lullaby" in sequence will develop a student's ability to play melody against accompaniment effectively. "By the Spring" may be used first to master balance between melody and accompaniment; "Lullaby" would follow, with particular attention to the duet between the hands.

Notice that here Gurlitt has given clear interpretive markings with ample slurs, dynamics, *crescendos* and *diminuendos*, and even the rarely seen instruction in m. 1 "*pronunziato il canto*" to emphasize the importance of making the melody sing out above the accompaniment. At the end, he stretches out the word *morendo*, giving added importance to the gradual dying away of the sound to **pp**.

Klage (Lament)

This dramatic solo has an element of defiance in it, as well as poignant sorrow. It is aptly titled, for a lament often signifies fresh sorrow at the loss of something dear, and this song has little in the way of comfort or resignation to loss in its character. As in the previous solo, this piece contains very clear indications concerning phrasing, dynamics,

and articulation. The *staccato* notes that conclude phrases 1, 3, 5, and 6 are particularly noteworthy. They abruptly cut off the *legato* line each time, causing these phrases to end with an abrupt, physical gesture, quite appropriate to the sentiment portrayed here.

I am struck by Gurlitt's masterful writing in this brief solo. Although the writing is simple, the dramatic effect is huge. Gurlitt achieves this dramatic richness by a combination of factors: the expressive key of F-sharp minor lends a dark color to the piece; the tempo indication *con moto* conveys urgency and is coupled with dynamics that lie between **mf** and **ff**, falling to **p** only at the very end; most importantly, a stark, single-note bass line enhances all the more the unsettled mood of the angular, disjunctive melody. A striking moment occurs at m. 32 where, having modulated earlier to the minor dominant, Gurlitt then slips back to the tonic key in one single, significant note—the B natural in the bass clef. The left-hand *crescendo* in this measure is central to an effective return to the tonic key, and may be further emphasized by using *rubato*.

Kirmes (The Fair)

Immediately likeable and easy to memorize, this carefree piece falls into that coveted category of "easy, sounds hard" solos, and is, therefore, a superb recital choice. The *Vivace* tempo and swirling, circular figures in the melody make it an excellent study in agility and flexibility, accessible even for the late-elementary student. The rapid 16th-note figures in the right hand have great flair, yet remain "under" the hand in a five-finger or slightly extended hand position.

In mm. 1-4 and similar measures, Gurlitt places slurs over the 16th-note and single eighth-note figures in the melody but does not extend the slurs to include the eighths that follow. I suggest playing the first three eighths following the slur *staccato* and the final one *portato* to give the melody greater interest.

Kirmes, Opus 101, No. 8: mm. 1-4, r.h.

I also recommend playing the left hand with a very light touch and varied *legato* and *staccato* articulation, keeping the fingers close to the keys for steady rhythmic control.

In the A-minor contrasting section, the division of the melody between the hands in mm. 14 and 16 may challenge inexperienced students, but attempting to redistribute these measures to give the right hand the entire melody makes the passage even more awkward. Rather, I encourage the performer to practice these passages slowly at first, and to note the *staccatos* on the right-hand eighths. These *staccato* notes are the key to playing the passage clearly.

Türkischer Marsch (Turkish March)

This little march opens with a cheerful E-major melody in which a dotted-eighth/16th motive figures prominently. Throughout the opening section, the dotted rhythms and rests must be exact to convey the spirit of Gurlitt's direction to play "*poco maestoso e marcato.*" In the left hand, the two-note slur that begins on the fourth beat of the measure each time (mm. 1-2, 2-3, 5-6, 6-7) deserves the performer's interest. This figure emphasizes the downbeat, and its upbeat start propels the line forward, acting as a musical thread that ties the measures together. No slurs are given in the source edition, but I have suggested one possibility with editorial slurs in the score.

The B section hints at the increasing musical and technical challenges to come. It is quite inventive, with a teasing melody set against a broken-chord accompaniment, and its musical sophistication marks a departure from the easier writing in the first part of the book. The indication *scherzando* and the *czardas*-like melody call for plenty of *rubato* and dynamic contrast.

This section also poses an intriguing editorial question: The final measure ends with a repeat sign, but there is no internal repeat at the expected place—the beginning of the B section. The A section unquestionably repeats, but does the B section? The answer is not clear. The repeat in the final measure may have been left there inadvertently when the A return was engraved in the original edition. This is a reasonable cause, but because the B section is such fun to play, I've elected to repeat it. Therefore, we have added an internal repeat editorially at m. 9.

Lied ohne Worte (Song Without Words)

The melody of this lovely song in ABA form unfolds in smooth four-bar phrases over a broken-chord accompaniment. Pay careful attention to the phrasing details here. The two-note slurs in mm. 13-14, 28-29, and 45-46 give the otherwise unchanging phrase lengths a needed variation. The piece is in G major, and Gurlitt's exact repetition of the theme in the dominant makes it both instructional and easy to learn.

Walzer (Waltz)

This elegant waltz begins with a left-hand melody in a rich cello register. Gurlitt was undoubtedly aware that a traditional waltz-bass pattern might have been too difficult for young students to master because of its frequent register shifts. By giving the melody to the left hand, he could then assign a simple quarter-note accompaniment to the right hand (on beats two and three) that preserves the characteristic, lilting accompaniment pattern of a waltz.

When the melody shifts to the right hand at m. 17, Gurlitt announces this register change with a low C in the bass clef—the only note in the piece that requires a large leap in the left hand, and the sole note that is written on leger lines below the bass clef. Therefore, this unique low C becomes a significant moment in the piece, one worth savoring a bit with a slight, lingering touch, *poco rubato*, before moving on.

The minor-key B section is unsettled and more dramatic. Beginning at m. 43 in the right hand, the performer must shift registers by octaves, back and forth. This can present a technical challenge for novice pianists, but careful preliminary work will produce positive results.

Der kleine Wandersmann (The Little Wanderer)

Colorful writing characterizes this delightful solo in ABA form. It is perhaps the best recital piece in the book and will appeal to students of all ages. The carefree title invites the performer to create a story to go along with the melody. Throughout the beginning section, the melody features the same four-bar pattern: a very short motive repeats and then lengthens to complete the phrase. This imparts a "whistling" character to the melody, and the motives within each phrase should be tossed off with happy abandon.

In the B section, the sturdy, *f* thirds in both hands give the player excellent technical practice: Playing these thirds exactly together with a vibrant pulse and a robust touch in both hands clearly feels good. This passage might very well be a younger student's first delicious taste of "virtuoso" writing,—a challenge that he or she can proudly master by playing these double-note leaps with confidence and freedom.

Grossvaters Geburtstag (Grandfather's Birthday)

A short celebratory work, "Grandfather's Birthday" is set in E-flat major, a key not often used in books for novice students, which makes it a very useful teaching piece. The distinguished character of this solo, with its opening and closing fanfares and full chords in mm. 21-27, promotes the development of a rich, round sound. Full chords are used here for the first time: Students with small hands may need to omit the upper notes of the left-hand chords in mm. 21-27. Judicious use of the damper pedal will enhance the quality of the chord passages, fanfares, and the tolling bell in mm. 29-31. It is curious that this bell tolls only three times—perhaps it rings for each score of years that the grandfather has lived!

The song itself, which begins just after the opening fanfare, is a familiar tune to those who know the nursery song "Down by the Station." Many of our favorite nursery songs owe their existence to their folk-song ancestors, and so it is possible to surmise that this melody originated as a German folk song that Gurlitt knew and incorporated into this piece. I could not find a folk-song source with the same melody to confirm my educated guess, but many young children do know the nursery song I mention above, and so this lovely piano solo will be a welcome treat.

Valse Noble

This evanescent waltz, whose sophistication is second only to the later "Schwärmerei," has a delicate, mercurial beauty. The graceful phrases fall under the hand with an easy, fluid sensation. Because of its subtle musical character, students should study this piece only after sufficiently honing their interpretive skills, especially the use of *tempo rubato*. Its mood calls to mind the more intimate mazurkas of Chopin in many places. Its phrasing exhibits the same detailed sculpting as those works, although this piece unfolds on a much smaller scale than those famous works.

The tentative opening gives way to a more confident, but still supple line in mm. 10-17. Here, the tempo may press forward a bit in response to the change in mood from *grazioso* to *scherzando*. This eight-bar phrase is noteworthy for its repeated emphasis on the second beat of the measure. The inventive accompaniment further accentuates this lovely syncopation. Students should practice these measures in groups of two, adding two measures with each repeat, so that gradually they may work up to playing a continuous, flowing phrase, straight through to m. 17, beat two.

Verlust (Loss)

Schumann's "First Loss" in his *Album for the Young* tells a story of loss and sorrow from a child's point of view. Gurlitt's exploration of the same emotion here resembles that well-known composition in many ways: The almost identical title and character, E-minor key signature, 2/4 meter, two-voice writing, and even Gurlitt's use of *portato* articulation lead one to believe that he surely must have known his colleague's famous album quite well.

The poignant melody, especially when it descends into a resonant tenor register in mm. 9-16, readily holds a listener's interest despite much repetition. Young students may welcome advice about varying repeated material so that their performances will keep the listener engaged to the very end. For this reason, "Loss" is a fine piece to use when teaching the concept of musical architecture, and showing how subtle inflections in the phrasing, varied dynamics or timbre (using the *una corda* pedal, perhaps), and even slight tempo fluctuations can make the same phrase sound quite new.

Scherzo

This spirited scherzo in E minor presents an arresting contrast to the previous work's somber mood. In that work, many characteristics point to Schumann's influence, but here, the sprightly, elfish personality of this piece reasonably suggests that Gurlitt may have been influenced by Grieg as well, for this work brings to mind Grieg's "Elfin Dance," also in the key of E minor.

Notwithstanding its minor key, this solo displays high energy and a sense of mischievous fun. The short motives will sparkle with a crisp, fresh ring if they are played with the tips of the fingers. Keeping the fingers close to the keys and cupping the hand slightly over each group of notes will help achieve just the right sound. Careful observation of the *staccato* notes, and those that are <u>not</u> *staccato*, will contribute to the liveliness of this puckish solo.

The B section in E major settles into a calmer, somewhat meandering style. The melody's chromaticism and the three-voice writing give the line much color, while the two-note slurs impart a playful character that echoes the sprightly personality of the opening, but in a gentler guise. The surprising leap to the high B at m. 79 signals the return of the A section and is an especially pleasing moment. Make the most of this delicious leap and the suspenseful mood it engenders.

A brief, reminiscent coda (mm. 117-133), marked *perdendosi*, fades away into the distance, trailing off to a full, sustained **pp** chord at the very end. Students with smaller hands may use the damper pedal here to sustain the notes in the left hand, but if they can hold the filled-in octave without straining, so much the better.

Schwärmerei (Passing Fancies)

This rich solo is the most sophisticated work in Gurlitt's *Albumleaves* and displays masterly writing. The work's brevity makes its near perfection all the more enchanting. Its expressive subtleties call for musical and technical maturity, placing it far beyond the scope of younger students.

The melody's buoyant phrases repeatedly begin on the weak beat of the measure and never quite resolve, inviting the listener to follow the melody with eager interest to discover where it will go. The flowing eighth-note accompaniment intensifies this effect: its constant eighths form a continuous stream of sound that carries the melody along without pause from the very first measure to the conclusion of the piece. The fluctuating harmonies and implied melody in the accompaniment also contribute to the intricate nature of this solo. These elements call for a very refined touch and ample use of the damper and *una corda* pedals throughout.

In mm. 9-23 the melody's constantly shifting rhythms set against the unchanging accompaniment make this passage especially intriguing. Giving subtle emphasis to certain notes in each hand with gentle stress, accents, or a slight *rubato* will enhance the subtle variations in each of the four phrases here. I've added accents and *tenuto* symbols to the examples below to illustrate these inflections. The first phrase (mm. 9-12) is simple and straightforward, with a slight accent on each downbeat:

Schwärmerei, Opus 101, No. 17: mm. 9-12

In the second phrase (mm. 13-16) the single-note melody always falls on the second half of the measure in a simple syncopation:

Schwärmerei, Opus 101, No. 17: mm. 13-16

In the third phrase (mm. 17-20) Gurlitt ornaments the melody of the previous phrase, turning the single notes into three-note slurs:

Schwärmerei, Opus 101, No. 17: mm. 17-20

In the last phrase (mm. 21-29) a true syncopation appears in the melody, highlighted by the unusual notation, beamed eighths across the bar. This passage ushers in the return of the opening theme, unanticipated and transformed from its opening *p espressivo* sentiment into an *appassionato f* statement. The effect is striking.

Schwärmerei, Opus 101, No. 17: mm. 21-29

"Schwärmerei" signals a shift in Gurlitt's creative focus, reflected in the *Albumleaves* that follow as well, from pedagogical studies for intermediate-level students to mature solos for accomplished, advancing pianists. This beautiful solo should be reserved for advancing students who have mastered the art of continuous, smooth *legato* and who possess a clear understanding of how harmony can determine where to place nuances within phrases.

Sonntag (Sunday)

"Sonntag" is a rather complex finger-legato study disguised as a peaceful song and chorale-tune setting, and it poses an excellent challenge for the advancing student. Like "Schwärmerei," this piece should not be assigned to intermediate students too soon in their studies.

The alternate fingering in parenthesis for the opening phrase will elicit the smoothest finger-legato, but it is more difficult than the primary fingering. Students may wish to learn both fingerings and then choose the one they can play most easily. As students work on developing a fine finger-legato, encourage them to think of their fingers as though they had no bones, or that their fingers are flexible noodles; the characteristic "crab-stepping" motion that is integral to this skill may then become easier to sense.

Advancing students must master another sophisticated technical challenge here, related to pedaling the *portato* notes in the left hand. The pedal release must come early enough to allow

the *portato* articulation to be heard, but the performer also must be ready to depress the pedal again, almost immediately, to help sustain the continuously *legato* right-hand melody. The performer cannot make this complex line completely *legato* by using fingers alone; the pedal also must come into play. And so two disparate touches command the performer's full attention here: the *portato* in the left hand, and the *legato* in the right. I have added editorial pedal to the first six measures to show how a precise application and release of the damper pedal can fulfill both needs. These important small details require careful listening skills, too.

Finally, in the second half of this solo, the finger-legato and sophisticated pedal technique learned in the first part may now be transferred directly to the chorale, with its four-voice, chordal writing.

Jagdstück (Hunting Song)

Gurlitt uses the traditional "hunting horn" key of E-flat major for this animated hunting song. Horn calls announce the opening of the piece, and a lively, cantering melody alternating between the hands ensues, characterized by repeated-note chords in a strong rhythmic pattern and punctuated by more horn calls.

When we compare this exciting solo to "March," the very first piece in the collection, it is easy to see at a glance the well-planned, progressive nature of this set of pieces. "March," a late-elementary solo, has the same confident spirit as this lively piece, but the resemblance ends there.

Salto Mortale (Aerial Somersault)

In circus parlance, a *"salto mortale"* is an aerial somersault. Knowing the meaning of this specialized term makes this dynamic character piece even more fascinating. Gurlitt conveys the precarious nature of an aerial somersault aptly: The expressive G-minor key, a leaping, arpeggiated melody, and mincing phrases interspersed throughout all create a sense of daring skill and breathless excitement.

The B section in the parallel key of G major has a reckless quirkiness. Its wide, arching leaps and angular phrasing may present an interpretive challenge to novice players. However, if one keeps in mind the image of an aerialist stepping lightly across a tightrope in preparation for another daring somersault, the pianist can conjure up, musically, the insouciant confidence of a supreme showman balanced on a slender wire high above a spellbound audience.

The arpeggios throughout must bound upward with a confident swing, and the mincing phrase that follows these arpeggios should be played with a dancing, athletic feel. Although the very widely spaced intervals in the B part were given to the right hand alone in the Schirmer source score, I have redistributed them between the hands. It might be appropriate, however, to attempt these leaps on the keyboard with only one hand to mimic more precisely the precarious nature of a high-wire performance. These notes certainly become much riskier when played with one hand. If one does attempt this, well-developed eye/hand coordination is needed for success—the performer must memorize the notes first, and then look ahead and at the keyboard, sizing up each note in the widely spaced intervals so that each leap is calculated in advance. A subtle use of *tempo rubato* here will also lend an air of daring tension to the execution of the leaps.

Programming Suggestions

The progressive nature of the solos in Gurlitt's *Albumleaves for the Young* makes this collection an ideal one for students to study in its entirety. Taken together, these expressive character pieces provide valuable technical instruction to the advancing pianist, promote the development of a fine musical sensitivity, and provide a fine introduction to the genre. Even so, I encourage pianists and teachers to consider including several contrasting solos in recital programs. Because an audience will not know these lovely solos as well as other Romantic character pieces, their inclusion in a recital program will be refreshingly welcome. The tempo suggestions and timings listed in the chart below will assist the performer in making programming choices.

—Margaret Otwell

Tempo/Timing Chart

Title	Tempo Range	Timing
Marsch (March)	♩ = 132-138	00:41
Morgengebet (Morning Prayer)	♩ = 58-63	01:18
Heiterer Morgen (A Sunshiny Morning)	♩ = 120-132	00:45
Nordische Klänge (Northern Strains)	♩ = 132-144	01:02
An der Quelle (By the Spring)	♩ = 108-116	00:48
Schlummerlied (Lullaby)	♩ = 104-108	01:00
Klage (Lament)	♩ = 132-144	00:27
Kirmes (The Fair)	♩ = 126-132	00:53
Türkischer Marsch (Turkish March)	♩ = 116-120	01:26
Lied ohne Worte (Song Without Words)	♩. = 80-84	00:42
Walzer (Waltz)	♩. = 72-76	01:48
Der kleine Wandersmann (The Little Wanderer)	♩. = 116-120	01:25
Grossvaters Geburtstag (Grandfather's Birthday)	♩ = 76-84	01:06
Valse Noble	♩ = 116	01:10
Verlust (Loss)	♩ = 84	01:08
Scherzo	♩. = 100-108	01:42
Schwärmerei (Passing Fancies)	♩. = 104	00:49
Sonntag (Sunday) (Chorale: ♩ = 96)	♩. = 44	01:41
Jagdstück (Hunting Song)	♩ = 104-112	01:10
Salto Mortale (Aerial Somersault)	♩ = 138	01:35

Marsch
March

C. Gurlitt
Op. 101, No. 1

Morgengebet
Morning Prayer

C. Gurlitt
Op. 101, No. 2

Heiterer Morgen

A Sunshiny Morning

C. Gurlitt
Op. 101, No. 3

Nordische Klänge
Northern Strains

C. Gurlitt
Op. 101, No. 4

An der Quelle
By the Spring

C. Gurlitt
Op. 101, No. 5

Moderato, quasi Allegretto

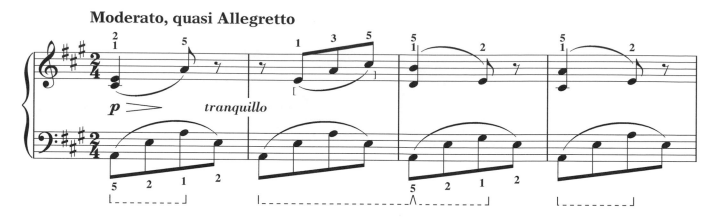

p *tranquillo*

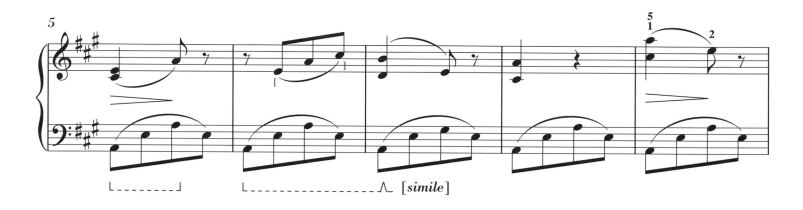

[simile]

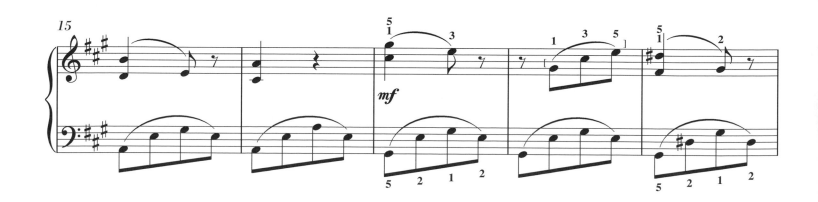

mf

per - den - do - si

Schlummerlied
Lullaby

C. Gurlitt
Op. 101, No. 6

Moderato

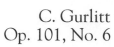
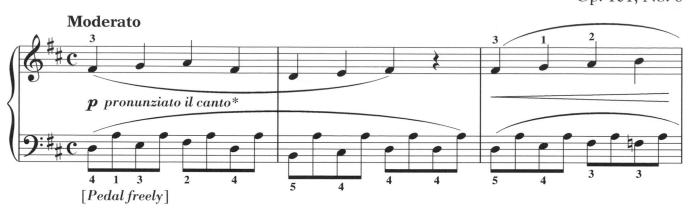

p pronunziato il canto*

[Pedal freely]

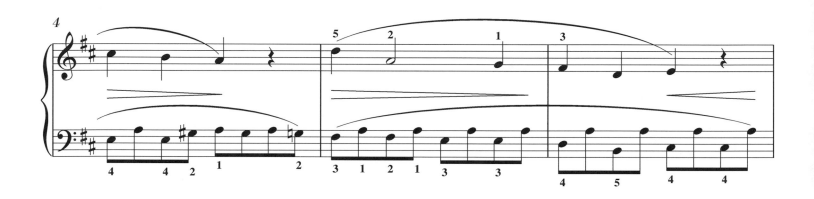

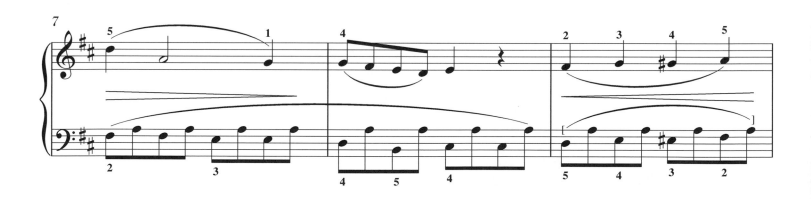

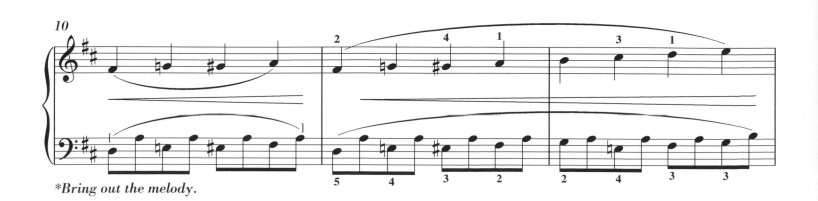

*Bring out the melody.

Klage
Lament

C. Gurlitt
Op. 101, No. 7

Kirmes
The Fair

C. Gurlitt
Op. 101, No. 8

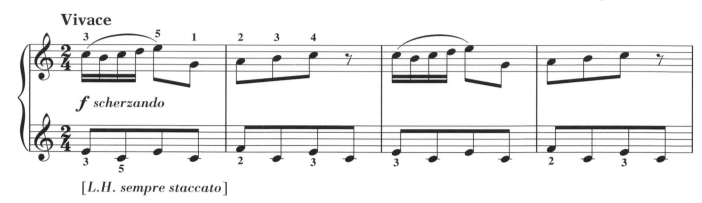

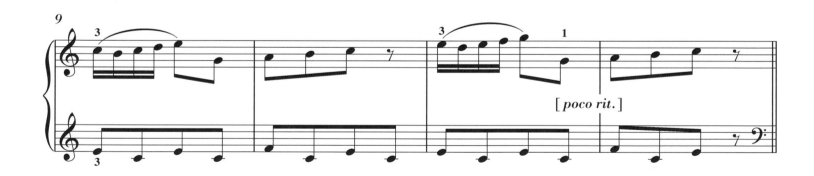

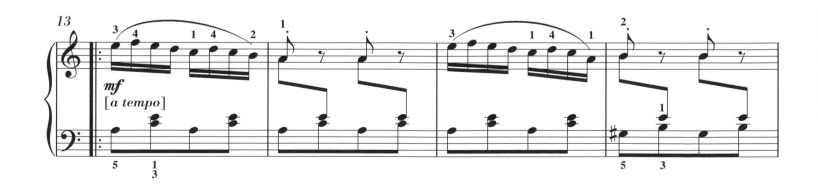

Türkischer Marsch

Turkish March

C. Gurlitt
Op. 101, No. 9

[Tempo Primo]

[poco rit.]

Lied ohne Worte

Song Without Words

C. Gurlitt
Op. 101, No. 10

Andantino

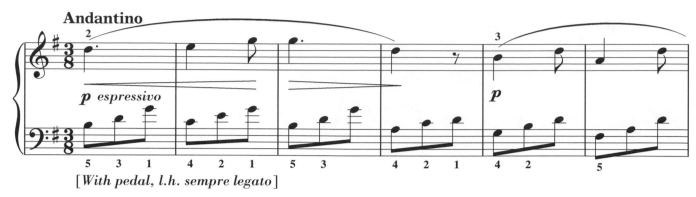

p espressivo

[*With pedal, l.h. sempre legato*]

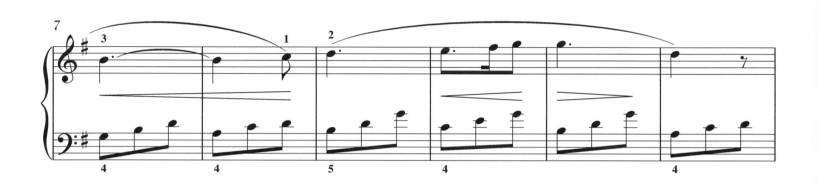

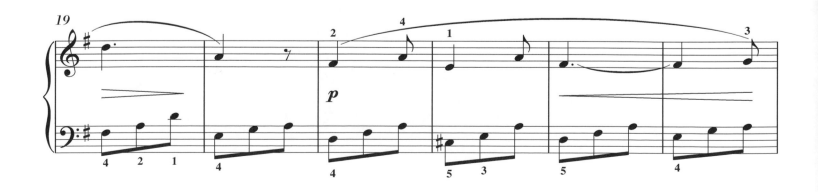

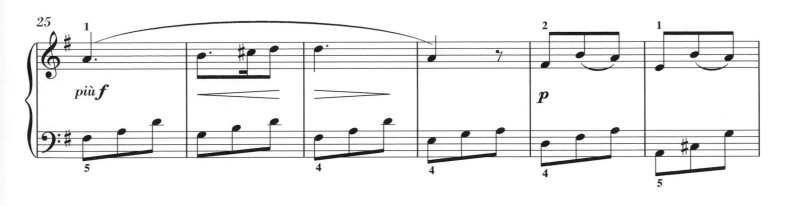

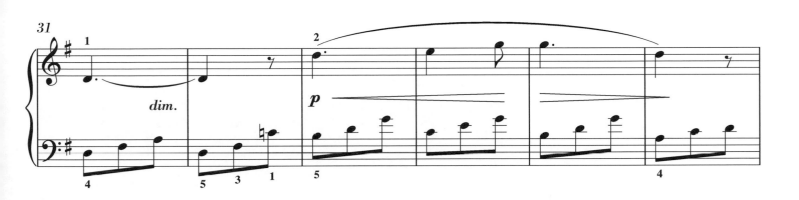

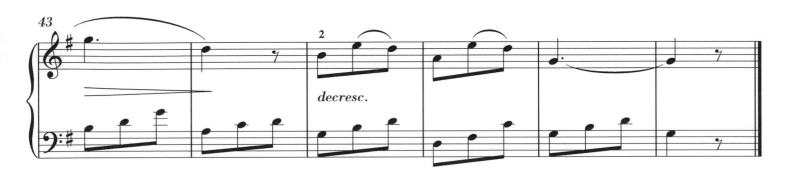

Walzer
Waltz

C. Gurlitt
Op. 101, No. 11

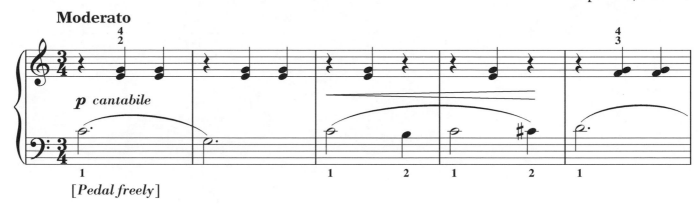

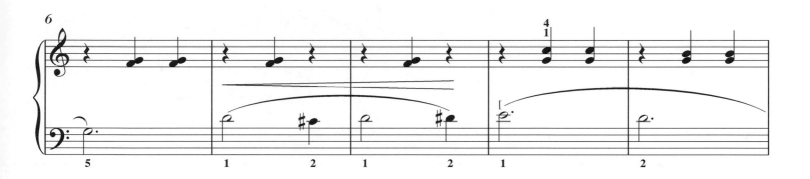

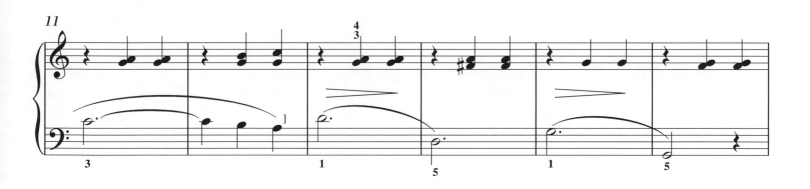

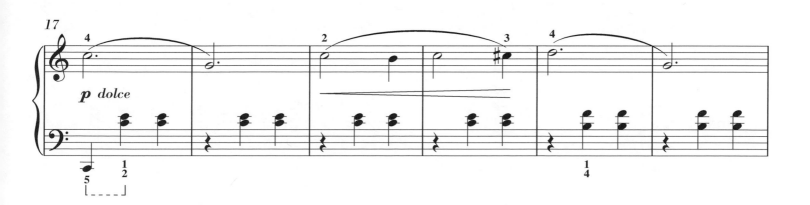

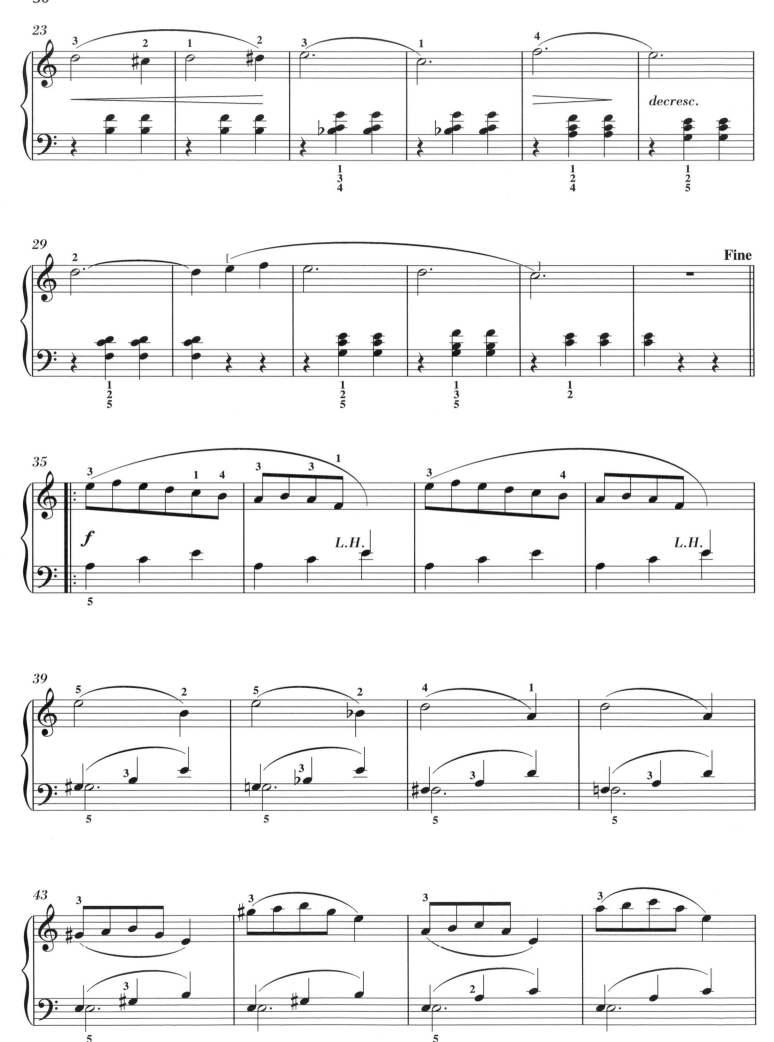

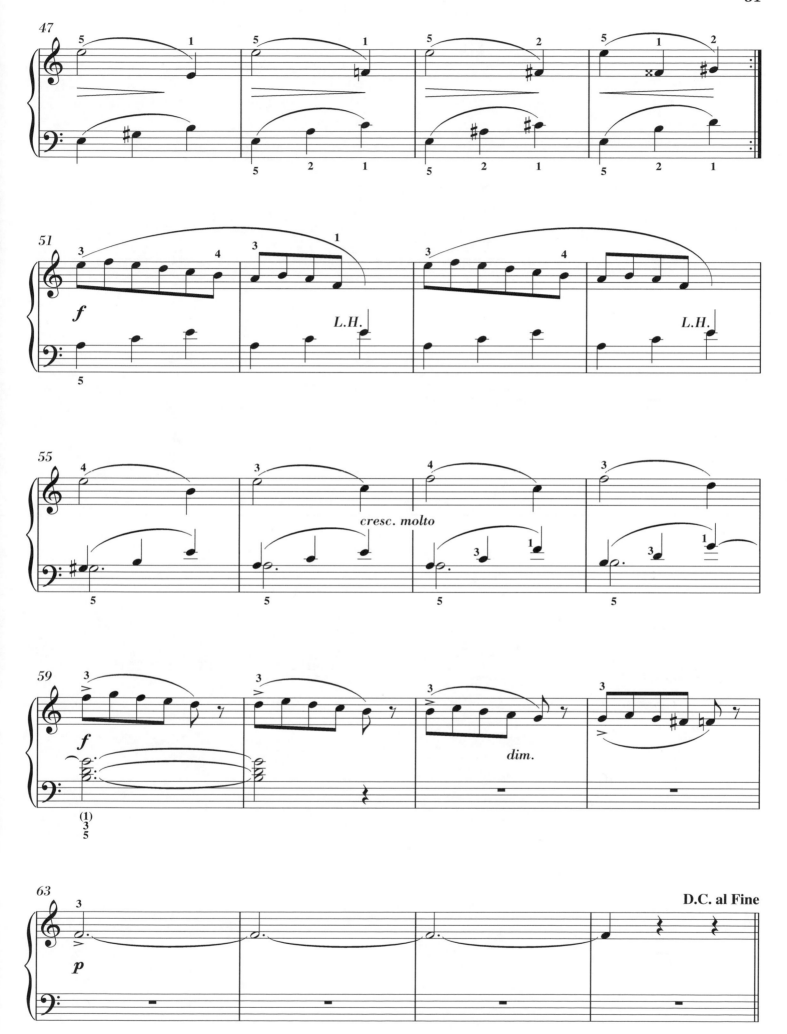

Der kleine Wandersmann
The Little Wanderer

C. Gurlitt
Op. 101, No. 12

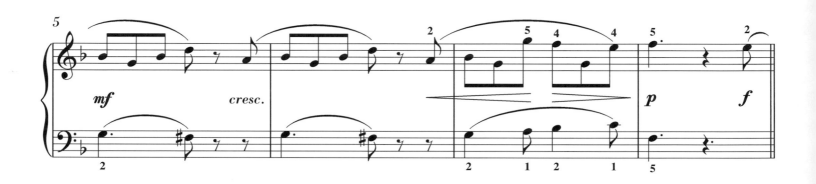

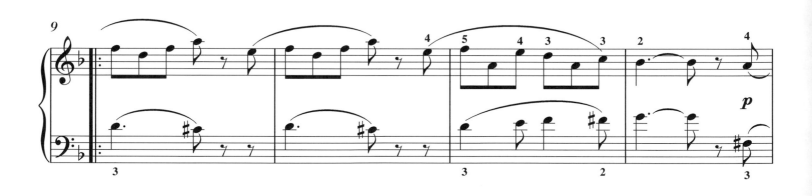

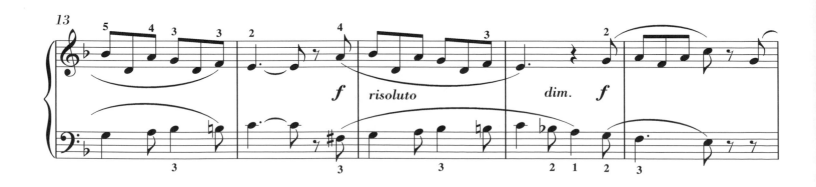

Grossvaters Geburtstag
Grandfather's Birthday

C. Gurlitt
Op. 101, No. 13

Mm. 21-24: Students with smaller hands may play only the bottom two notes of the L.H. chords.

Valse Noble

C. Gurlitt
Op. 101, No. 14

Verlust
Loss

C. Gurlitt
Op. 101, No. 15

Andante con espressione

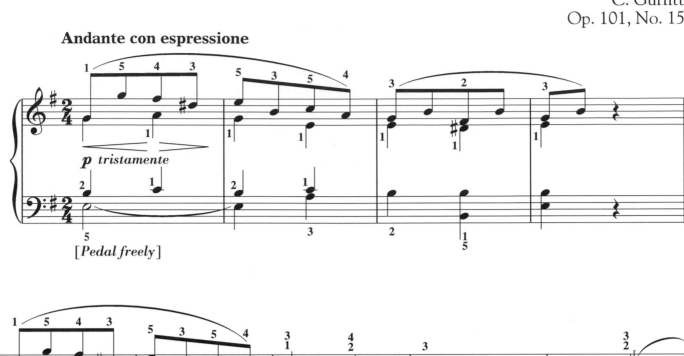

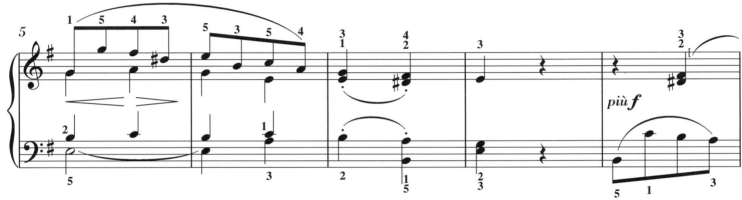

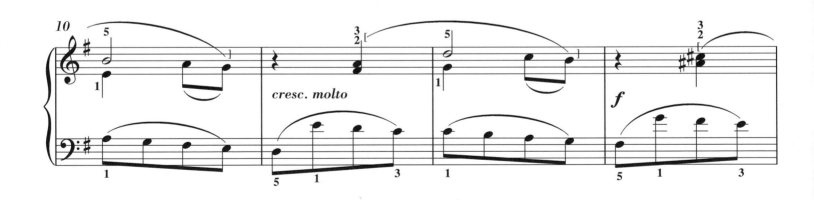

Scherzo

C. Gurlitt
Op. 101, No. 16

Schwärmerei
Passing Fancies

C. Gurlitt
Op. 101, No. 17

Sonntag
Sunday

C. Gurlitt
Op. 101, No. 18

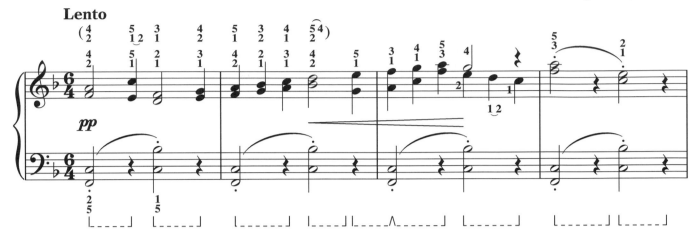

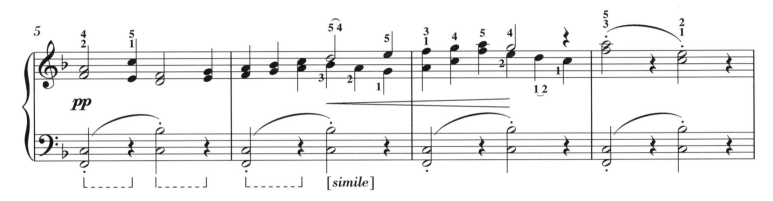

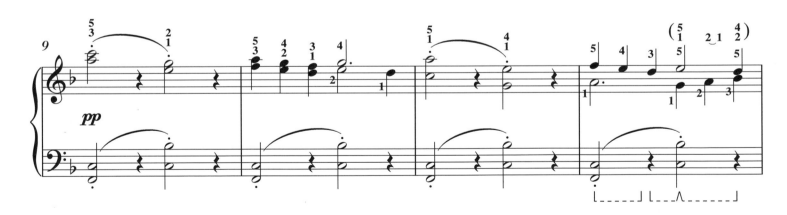

47

Choral { *Lobe den Herren, den mächtigen König der Ehren.*
{ Praise to the Lord, the Almighty, the King of Glory.

Jagdstück

Hunting Song

C. Gurlitt
Op. 101, No. 19

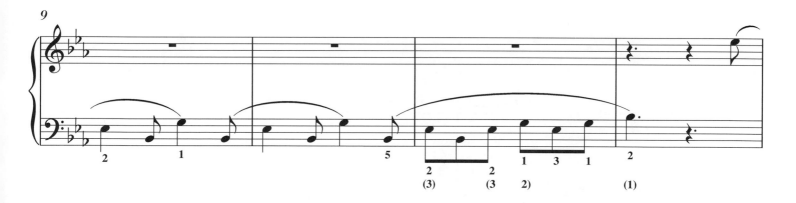

Salto Mortale
Aerial Somersault

C. Gurlitt
Op. 101, No. 20

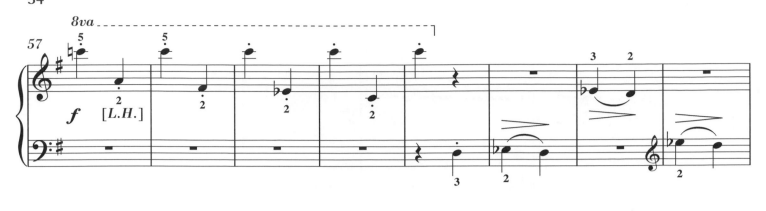

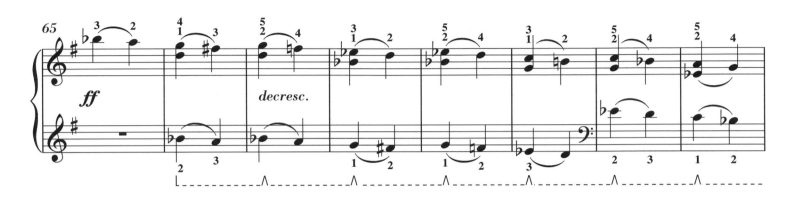

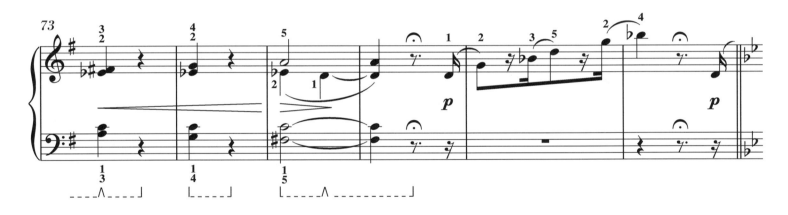

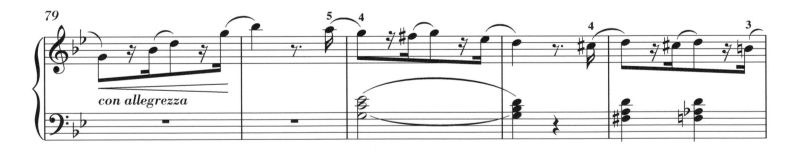

ABOUT THE EDITOR

MARGARET OTWELL

Margaret Otwell is a musician with a distinguished and varied career as a solo pianist, collaborative musician, and teacher. She has pursued an active role in educating young pianists as an independent piano teacher for over 25 years. A member of MTNA since 1978, she is a past president of the Northern Virginia Music Teachers Association, and has adjudicated for many piano competitions and events, including the Wolf Trap Young Artist Competition in Washington, DC and the National Piano Arts Competition in Milwaukee, WI. Dr. Otwell has served on the faculties of the University of Maryland Eastern Shore, The American University Preparatory Department, and George Mason University. She is currently Director of Educational Keyboard Publications for Hal Leonard Corporation in Milwaukee.

As a pianist, Dr. Otwell is well known for her insightful interpretation of French piano repertoire. She has recorded the complete works of Déodat de Séverac for Musical Heritage Society Records. She has presented lecture-recitals, workshops, and master classes and has appeared in solo and chamber music performances throughout the United States, Canada, and Europe. Dr. Otwell was awarded a DMA degree in Performance from the University of Maryland, where she studied piano and pedagogy with Stewart Gordon, Thomas Schumacher, and Nelita True. She also studied piano with Gaby Casadesus as a recipient of a Fulbright performance grant to France.